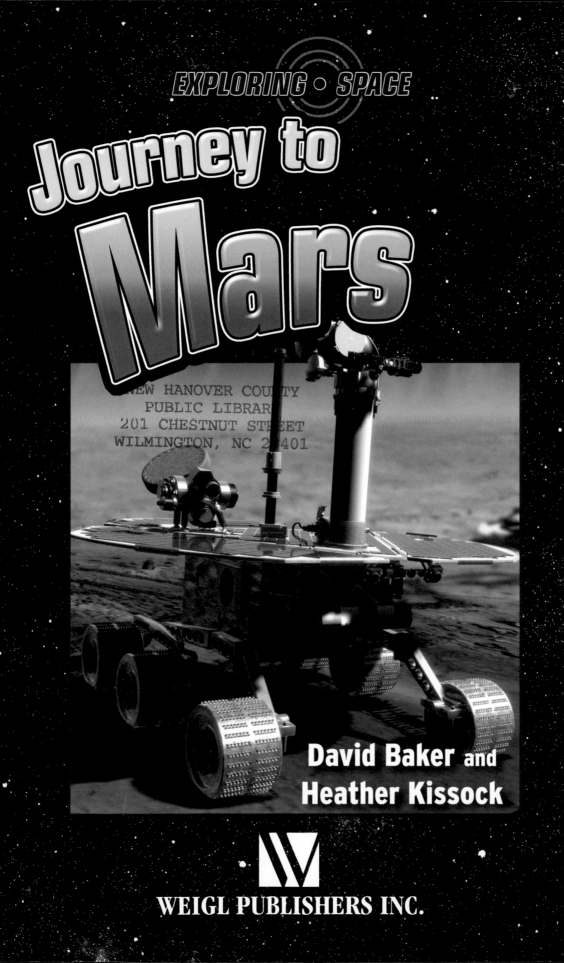

EXPLORING · SPACE

Journey to Mars

David Baker and **Heather Kissock**

WEIGL PUBLISHERS INC.

Published by Weigl Publishers Inc.
350 5th Avenue, Suite 3304, PMB 6G
New York, NY 10118-0069

Website: www.weigl.com

Library of Congress Cataloging-in-Publication Data

Baker, David, 1944-
 Journey to Mars / David Baker and Heather Kissock.
    p. cm.
 Includes index.
 ISBN 978-1-60596-029-6 (hard cover : alk. paper) --
 ISBN 978-1-60596-030-2 (soft cover : alk. paper)
 1. Mars (Planet)--Juvenile literature. 2. Mars (Planet)--Geology--Juvenile literature. I. Kissock, Heather. II. Title.

 QB641.B228 2010
 523.43--dc22

                            2008052055

Printed in China
1 2 3 4 5 6 7 8 9 0 13 12 11 10 09

Weigl would like to acknowledge Getty Images and NASA as its primary photo suppliers for this title.

EDITOR: Heather Kissock
DESIGN: Terry Paulhus

Journey to Mars

CONTENTS

04   The Fourth Planet
06   Mars Explorers
08   A Planet of Interest
10   Mars from Space
12   Touchdown on Mars
14   A New Plan
16   The Little Rover that Could
18   A Renewed Interest
20   New Ways to Explore
22   Making the Grade
24   A Day in Space
26   Footprints on Mars
28   Test Your Knowledge
30   Further Resources
31   Glossary
32   Index

The Fourth Planet

On a cloudless night, the planet Mars can be seen clearly with the naked eye. It appears as a reddish light, shining like a bright star. Mars is sometimes called the "red planet" because of its reddish hue.

Mars is the fourth planet from the Sun. After Venus, it is the planet closest to Earth. Mars is much smaller than Earth in size, but the two planets share many traits. In fact, scientists believe that, at one time, Mars had a similar environment to Earth.

Its closeness to Earth has encouraged many **theories** about what Mars is like. People through time have held the belief that the planet was home to living beings. This belief was promoted by many science fiction writers, who created an imaginary world inhabited by beings called Martians. As space technology developed, these stories were proven to be baseless. Scientists have not yet found evidence of life on Mars. Still, the idea that there could be life there encouraged scientists to find ways to get close to the planet and even to land on it. As a result, Mars is one of the most explored planets in the **solar system**.

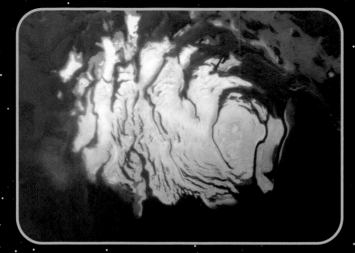

Mars has ice sheets on its North and South Poles. This has led scientists to believe that some life forms may have existed on the planet at one time.

H.G. Wells book *The War of the Worlds* is about a Martian invasion. The book has been used to make two movies, one in 1953, and a more recent one in 2005.

BRAIN BOOSTER

Mars has a great deal of **iron oxide** in its surface dust. This is what gives the planet its reddish color.

Stories about Martians were popular in the early twentieth century. Authors such as H.G. Wells, Edgar Rice Burroughs, and Ray Bradbury created stories based on these space aliens.

Mars
Explorers

Humans have yet to step on Mars. Instead, scientists have sent a variety of spacecraft to the planet to take pictures and run tests. These spacecraft include three types of space probes and a robotic vehicle called a rover.

1 FLYBY PROBE

Flyby probes take readings and pictures of space bodies as they fly past them. These probes only study the space body for a few hours and usually only focus on one area.

2 ORBITER PROBE

An orbiter probe stays with the planet for a longer period. It orbits, or circles, the body, taking pictures and readings of the area the orbit covers.

3 LANDER PROBE

Lander probes actually touch down on the planet or space body. This allows for more detailed research on the environment. Landers stay in the place where they landed for their entire mission.

ROVER

Rovers are vehicles brought to a space body by a lander probe. The lander probe releases them, and they then travel over the terrain of the body. They can then gather detailed information about different parts of the planet or space body.

A Planet
of Interest

Human fascination with Mars began many centuries ago. Probably because of its reddish color, the **Babylonians** named it Nergal, after the god of fire and destruction. Its modern name of Mars came from the Romans, who named it after their god of war.

Since the invention of the telescope in 1609, scientists have been looking at Mars in more detail. One feature they noticed early in their studies was a series of straight lines running over the planet's surface. The scientists of the time believed that these lines were **irrigation canals**. They thought that beings similar to humans must have lived on Mars and built the structures.

Scientists also saw light and dark patches move across the surface of the planet. Some scientists believed that these were seasonal changes, like those that occur on Earth. Other scientists thought these patches were plants that grew in the spring and died in the fall. They suggested that the plants were being grown by living beings, who would sow seeds in the spring and harvest crops in the summer. This theory promoted the idea that life existed on Mars. Over time, the idea of a Martian civilization became part of **popular culture**.

A scientist named Percival Lowell drew pictures of the canals he thought he saw. He later published them in a book.

As a result, Mars became a priority destination when space travel first became possible. After the first probe successfully reached the Moon, scientists focused their attention on the red planet. The first probe was sent to Mars in 1964. Since then, at least 16 other spacecraft have successfully reached the planet, and more continue to be scheduled. While it is uncertain if Mars ever held life, scientists want to know if living beings could survive there today.

Scientists have observed ice clouds floating over the planet's surface. These may have been the color changes the earlier scientists noticed.

THINK ABOUT IT

Think about Earth's ability to sustain life. What features would Mars need to have for people to live there?

Mars
from Space

The first spacecraft sent to Mars was a **NASA** probe called Mariner 4. It was launched on November 28, 1964, and flew by Mars a few months later. As it did, it took 22 black and white pictures, which were sent back to Earth. The pictures proved that the planet did not have **extraterrestrial beings** living on it. Instead, the pictures showed Mars to have a barren, sandy landscape covered with **craters**. The canals that early scientists thought they had seen were an **optical illusion**. Still, Mariner's pictures indicated that water did flow on the planet at one time.

Mariner 4 was the first spacecraft to take closeup pictures of another planet.

In the following years, more Mariner probes were sent to Mars. Mariners 6 and 7 successfully reached their destination and, like Mariner 4, flew past Mars, taking hundreds of pictures of the red planet. However, these missions only provided a brief glimpse of the planet.

GET CONNECTED

To read more about the Mariner probe missions, go to http://history.nasa.gov/mariner.html.

In 1971, Mariner 9 was launched. This probe was an orbiter. When it reached Mars, it became the first probe to set a course around the planet. For almost a year, it circled the planet twice a day, taking thousands of pictures of seasonal changes and surface details.

Mariner 9's pictures helped scientists find out more about the surface of Mars. While orbiting the planet, Mariner 9 found several large volcanoes and a canyon that stretched 3,000 miles (4,800 kilometers) across the planet. It noted that the planet's North and South Poles were covered with ice. The probe did not find liquid water, but it took pictures of land formations that looked like riverbeds. This indicated that, at one time, water had flowed on the planet. As water is key to life, this discovery again raised the question about life on Mars. Scientists felt that the only way to find out if Mars could support life was to land a probe on the planet.

As part of its mission, Mariner 9 took the first detailed pictures of Mars' moons, including Phobos.

Touchdown
on Mars

In 1975, NASA sent two probes, Viking 1 and 2, to Mars. Like previous probes, the mission of these orbiters was to circle the planet and take pictures. Attached to each orbiter, however, was another part called a lander. Its mission was to detach from the orbiter and set down on the planet.

The two Viking landers touched down on different parts of Mars. Viking 1 landed in an area called Chryse Planitia, near a large canyon. This was where scientists thought there might have been shallow seas at one time. They were hopeful that **fossils** of ancient life forms might be found. Viking 2 landed on the other side of Mars. Here, the surface was strewn with rocks spewed by volcanoes long ago. Each lander carried a set of instruments to test soil samples for signs of life, but none were found.

The landers were only expected to work for six months. Both lasted much longer. Viking 2 worked for 5 years. Viking 1 stopped working after 7 years.

The Face on Mars

Children often play shadow puppets with their hands on a wall lit by candles. Folding fingers and thumbs into shapes such as rabbits with long ears, they bring shadows to life. Light can play tricks with the imagination. This occurred during the Viking missions to Mars.

One of the Viking orbiters sent back a picture of an object that looked like a human face. Some people believed that it was a sculpture that had been carved by an ancient Martian civilization. NASA received thousands of letters from people wanting the space agency to investigate the feature. Later, when other spacecraft took pictures over the same area, it was almost impossible to see any likeness to a human face. The effects of shadow and light had changed the look of the landscape, making it appear to be something that was not there.

The facelike landform extends about 2 miles (3.2 kilometers) from one end to the other.

A New Plan

During the 1980s, scientists were eager to send more spacecraft to Mars. However, as more parts were added to probes, the cost of making them and sending them into space increased. NASA could not afford to continue the missions as they were.

Scientists and engineers worked together to produce a new type of spacecraft that could be faster, better, and cheaper than those of the past. They used modern computers and technology to reduce the size and weight of each spacecraft and increase the amount of information they could send back.

In 1996, NASA sent two probes to Mars as part of this new program. One, called Mars Global Surveyor, entered Mars' orbit and took pictures of the surface. These would be used to map the planet over several years. To reduce the amount of fuel needed to operate the probe, scientists added a small braking rocket. Instead of using fuel to move into position, the probe used the **gravity** of Mars to pull it into orbit. As Surveyor sliced through Mars' **atmosphere**, the brake slowed the probe and gently lowered it into orbit. This technique is known as aerobraking.

About $250 million was saved by adding the small braking rocket to the Mars Global Surveyor. The mission saved on fuel costs, and the reduced fuel load allowed the probe to be launched using a smaller rocket as well.

The second spacecraft launched was Mars Pathfinder. Pathfinder was built as a lander probe. It was meant to land on Mars and gather information from the planet's surface. In the past, lander probes had been very expensive to operate. Many of them did not make successful landings, and were damaged or destroyed during the process. This added to the cost of the mission. To increase the chance of a safe landing, NASA's scientists attached airbags to the probe. This helped to prevent the vehicle from being damaged, and it reduced the amount of fuel needed to control the probe's braking rockets.

Mars Pathfinder's airbags cushioned the spacecraft's landing. The probe rested on the airbags after impact.

GET CONNECTED

To view images taken by Pathfinder on Mars, go to http://nssdc.gsfc.nasa.gov/planetary/marspath_images_2.html.

The Little Rover
that Could

The exploration of Mars could only really begin when robot spacecraft could land on the surface and move around. The orbiting spacecraft circling Mars had revealed much that scientists did not know about the planet. However, the closest look of all, from the surface, was the only way to get detailed information about conditions on the planet. Viking 1 and Viking 2 had landed on Mars in 1976, but they had stayed in specific locations on the planet. As a result, they were only able to give scientists information about those places.

When Mars Pathfinder landed on Mars in 1997, a new age in Mars exploration began. Pathfinder was actually two vehicles. Inside the lander was a small rover, called Sojourner. Sojourner's ability to move over the planet's surface allowed scientists to explore new places. The rover gathered information from different parts of the planet. This increased scientists' understanding of the planet's geology and the materials that form its surface.

Sojourner was sent to Mars to gather information on the planet's rocks and soil. Many of its pictures are of the planet's surface features.

Sojourner weighed only 23 pounds (11 kilograms). It was powered mainly by electricity produced from **solar cells**. This power operated the rover's motor and its communications system, which allowed scientists on Earth to send and receive information via radio signals. Sojourner's mission on Mars only lasted for three months. In that time, it sent 550 images of the planet to Earth. These images suggested that, at one time, Mars had a warm, moist climate.

Scientists have continued to develop more advanced rovers to send to Mars. One of the more recent rovers is called K-9. It will undergo much testing before it is sent into space.

BRAIN BOOSTER

Sojourner's maximum speed was about 0.4 inches (1 centimeter) per second.

Sojourner was named after Sojourner Truth, an African American who lived during the Civil War. Sojourner Truth fought for women's legal rights and the right of all people to be free.

A Renewed
Interest

The success of Sojourner led to the creation of more Mars rovers. In June and July 2003, NASA launched two more roving vehicles toward Mars. Each one was bigger, and designed to last longer, than the little Sojourner rover launched in 1996. Spirit and Opportunity were sent to Mars as part of NASA's Mars Exploration Rover program.

Called robotic geologists, their job was to research the history of water on Mars. Spirit landed on Mars on January 3, 2004, in a crater called Gusev. Scientists believe that Gusev may have been a lake at one time. Later that month, on January 24, Opportunity landed on the opposite side of Mars in a place called Meridiani Planum. Here, **mineral deposits** show that Mars had once been a moist planet.

Each rover was equipped with special instruments that could examine rocks and other materials on the planet's surface. One instrument measured the **chemical composition** of surface rocks. A robotic arm allowed the rover to pick up rocks. The rovers had a tool that could scrape away layers of rocks so that they could be studied on this inside. Spirit and Opportunity remain on Mars, where they continue to perform research for scientists on Earth. Both have shown scientists that Mars once had liquid water.

Both Spirit and Opportunity had special stereo cameras that allowed the rovers to get a "human eye" view of the surroundings.

Locating water on Mars is central to NASA's current space exploration program. Water plays a key role in supporting life and would help humans survive if they were to land there. Many vehicles are searching for water sources on the red planet.

The Mars Phoenix landing probe set down on the northern polar region of Mars in May 2008. It was sent to study the polar ice, as well as collect information on the planet's weather. Phoenix discovered that Mars receives snowfall. This shows moisture in the atmosphere.

The Mars Reconnaissance Orbiter's radar can probe up to 0.62 miles (1 km) below the planet's surface.

Another probe, the Mars Reconnaissance Orbiter, carried **radar** equipment to study beneath Mars' surface. Underneath many layers of rock, the probe found several huge **glaciers**. These glaciers could provide humans with a water source if they land on Mars. They may also contain fossils of life forms that once lived on the planet.

THINK ABOUT IT Spirit and Opportunity are both examining rocks to find out more about water on Mars. How can rocks provide information on water?

New Ways
to Explore

N ASA has been sending probes and rovers to Mars for many years. These spacecraft have provided scientists with much information about the planet and will continue to do so in the coming years. However, while these studies have been taking place, scientists have been developing new technology to take the research even further.

Scientists are currently working on plans to use airplanes in their study of the red planet. The airplane they are designing will not carry people. Instead, it will have its own **navigation** system, so it can steer itself around Mars. Scientists believe that airplanes will be able to gather more information about Mars than rovers and probes. This is because they can fly closer to the surface than an orbiter probe and cover more area than a rover.

Besides airplanes, scientists are also examining the role that balloons can play in gathering data from Mars.

At some point, scientists hope to create technology that allows probes to leave Mars and return to Earth with soil and rock samples, as well as other information.

Scientists are planning to send equipment to Mars that can go underground and explore the planet's subsurface. These robotic moles will be able to drill deep into the planet's surface, gathering soil samples at each stage of their journey. These samples will be sent to the surface using a long tube. Once at the surface, the samples will be analyzed by special **imaging** equipment to see what minerals are available underground. Currently, there is no way to bring the samples back to Earth for further study. Scientists are working on making rockets that could go to and from Mars for this purpose.

BRAIN BOOSTER

The robotic moles will be able to drill hundreds of yards (meters) into the ground. They will drill up to 66 feet (20 m) each day.

NASA hopes to create balloons that can float above the Mars' surface for up to 100 days, taking pictures and gathering other information.

Making
the Grade

Working with space probes and rovers requires people to have very specific skills and education. Probe and rover specialists must have a good grasp of science principles, along with strong technical skills. They must be detail-oriented people who strive to improve current technologies, With these traits and qualifications, there are many career paths that can be taken.

ASTRONAUTICAL ENGINEER

Astronautical engineers design, develop, and test spacecraft, including probes and rovers. They often specialize in very specific areas, such as structural design and navigation or communication systems. It is their job to create equipment and vehicles that can survive the journey from Earth to space and back again. They need to have expert knowledge on the conditions the equipment will experience so that the correct materials and technology are used to create it. They are involved in the construction process from design to finished product.

ASTRONAUT QUALIFICATIONS

CITIZENSHIP

Space shuttle pilots and **mission specialists** must be U.S. citizens. **Payload specialists** can be from other countries.

EDUCATION

Astronauts must have a minimum bachelor's degree in engineering, biology, physics, or mathematics. Most astronauts have a **doctorate**.

SOFTWARE ENGINEER

Software engineers make computer programs that operate inside the probes and rovers. These programs may help with the vehicle's navigation system or with the work that the vehicle is in space to do, such as measure magnetic fields and take soil samples. Once these programs are developed, the software engineer will make sure that they work properly, testing them from time to time, and correcting or improving any parts of the program that are not working well.

LAUNCH MANAGER

A launch manager is the person who prepares to launch a probe or rover into space. Launch managers schedule the launch process. The launch manager arranges for a launch vehicle, such as a rocket or space shuttle, to carry the probe into space. He or she must make sure that the vehicle is large enough and strong enough to carry the probe into space. Launch managers arrange to transport the probe to the launch site. They must have a good understanding of the probe development process, as well as NASA's safety standards, so that the launch process runs smoothly and safely.

EXPERIENCE	HEALTH	HEIGHT
Astronauts must have at least three years of experience in a science-related field. Pilots must have jet experience with more than 1,000 hours of in-command flight time.	All astronauts must pass a NASA physical, with specific vision and blood pressure requirements.	Pilots must be 64 to 76 inches (162.5 to 193 cm) tall. Mission or payload specialists must be 58.5 to 76 inches (148.5 to 193 cm) tall.

A Day
in Space

Space probes and other vehicles are often taken into space by a space shuttle. When a shuttle takes a probe into space, releasing it is just one job in a day that has a firmly set schedule, with certain tasks to be done at specific times. Flight controllers on Earth wake up the crew in the morning with a pop song that they blast over the shuttle's speakers. For breakfast, astronauts eat a meal that they chose before launch. After eating, it is time for the astronauts to get ready for work.

A list, known as the flight plan, tells the crew what they are to work on each day. Sometimes, there is the need for a spacewalk. Other times, the crew carries out housekeeping duties, such as trash collection and cleaning. Breaks, such as lunch and dinner, are scheduled throughout the day. Blocks of time are put aside for the astronauts to set up and use exercise equipment. At the end of the work day, the astronauts may read a book or listen to music.

The Daily Schedule

8:30 to 10:00 a.m.: Post-sleep (Morning station inspection, breakfast, morning **hygiene**)

10:00 to 10:30 a.m.: Planning and coordination (Daily planning conference and status report)

10:30 a.m. to 1:00 p.m.: Exercise (Set-up exercise equipment, exercise, and put equipment away)

1:00 to 2:00 p.m.: Lunch, personal hygiene

2:00 to 3:30 p.m.: Daily systems operations (Work preparation, report writing, emails, to-do list review, trash collection)

3:30 to 10:00 p.m.: Work (Work set-up and maintenance, performing experiments and payload operations, checking positioning and operating systems)

10:00 p.m. to 12:00 a.m.: Pre-sleep (food preparation, evening meal, and hygiene)

12:00 to 8:30 a.m.: Sleep

The work that astronauts do on the shuttle is serious, but there is always time to enjoy the experience of being in space.

Teamwork is an essential part of space shuttle life.
Astronauts live in a confined space for days. They must all work together to make the trip comfortable for everyone on board.

Footprints
on Mars

The ultimate goal of NASA's Mars Exploration Program is to put humans on the planet. Currently, NASA, the Russian Space Agency, and the European Space Agency are all planning to send people to Mars. It is estimated that this will occur around the year 2030.

Before people can land on Mars, however, scientists must be able to ensure their safety. One of the main concerns scientists have about Mars is the level of **radiation** found there. Unlike Earth, Mars does not have an ozone layer to protect it from the Sun's **ultraviolet rays**. Before humans can go to Mars, scientists must determine how much radiation Mars receives and design spacesuits and other equipment to counter it.

A research station has been set up in Utah to test equipment and clothing that can be used for human missions to Mars.

Once all the studies have taken place and the proper equipment created, human missions will begin taking place. The first missions will be for short periods, much like the few hours that humans first spent on the Moon. Over time, however, scientists hope to build a research station on Mars. This will allow astronauts to stay on the planet for longer periods and perform more in-depth research and experiments. The Mars research station will be similar to the base NASA is planning to build on the Moon by 2024.

Space Base

In January 2004, President George W. Bush announced that NASA was going to begin a new age in space exploration. Astronauts are to return to the Moon and then travel farther into space to planets such as Mars. The goal is to find other space bodies capable of supporting human life.

Astronauts are to return to the Moon by 2020 to begin building a permanent settlement there. This Moon base is to include housing, laboratories, and vehicles. It will be a place where astronauts can stay for periods up to six months and perform long-term studies. The base will be as self-sufficient as possible. Its power will come mainly from solar panels. Its oxygen is to be taken from the Moon's soil. There is even a plan to have a greenhouse on the Moon so that astronauts can grow their own food. Once this is achieved, the Moon base will be used as the **prototype** for bases on other planets and space bodies, including Mars.

NASA has targeted Mars to be the first planet, after Earth, to have a research station built on it.

Test Your
Knowledge

1 What causes Mars to look red?

Iron oxide in its surface dust

2 Name three types of space probe.

Flyby, orbiter, and lander

3 Who is Mars named after?

The Roman god of war

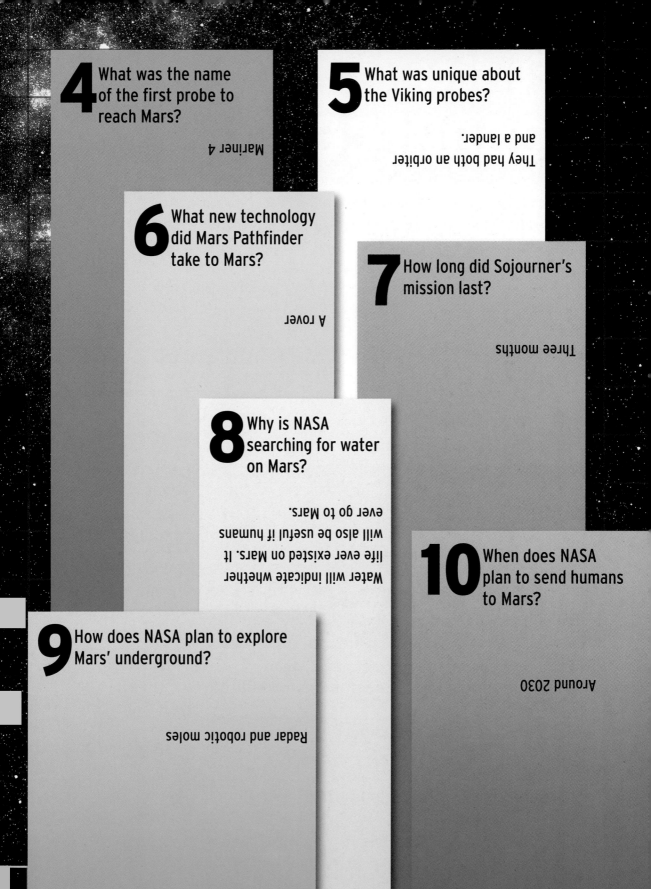

4 What was the name of the first probe to reach Mars?

Mariner 4

5 What was unique about the Viking probes?

They had both an orbiter and a lander.

6 What new technology did Mars Pathfinder take to Mars?

A rover

7 How long did Sojourner's mission last?

Three months

8 Why is NASA searching for water on Mars?

Water will indicate whether life ever existed on Mars. It will also be useful if humans ever go to Mars.

9 How does NASA plan to explore Mars' underground?

Radar and robotic moles

10 When does NASA plan to send humans to Mars?

Around 2030

Further
Resources

Many books provide information on space exploration. To learn more about what lies beyond Earth's atmosphere, try reading these books.

Lomberg, Michelle. *Mars*. New York, NY: Weigl Publishers Inc., 2004.

Lomberg, Michelle. *Planets*. New York, NY: Weigl Publishers Inc., 2003.

Willett, Edward. *Space*. New York, NY: Weigl Publishers Inc., 2010.

Websites

To find out more about the red planet, go to **www.astronomytoday.com/astronomy/mars.html**.

Build a model of Mars Pathfinder by visiting **http://marsprogram.jpl.nasa.gov/ MPF/mpf/education/cutouts.html**.

Learn more about NASA's Mars Exploration Program at **http://marsweb.jpl.nasa.gov**.

Glossary

atmosphere: the layer of gases that surrounds a planet

Babylonians: an ancient people that once lived in the area now known as Iraq

chemical composition: the substances that make up an object

craters: bowl-shaped openings in the ground

doctorate: an advanced university degree

extraterrestrial beings: life forms that do not originate on Earth

fossils: the remains of an organism from the past

glaciers: slow-moving sheets of ice

gravity: a force that pulls things toward the center of a planet

hygiene: the process of keeping clean

imaging: the process of creating pictures

iron oxide: a naturally occurring substance that is red in color

irrigation canals: a humanmade channel used to transport water

mineral deposits: a mass of naturally occurring rocks and ores

mission specialists: scientists sent into space by NASA

NASA: National Aeronautics and Space Administration; the United States' civilian agency for research into space and aviation

navigation: the act of directing or plotting a path

optical illusion: something that tricks the eye

payload specialist: scientists sent into space by companies or countries other than the United States

popular culture: the beliefs and customs of a specific age and people

prototype: an original design that serves as a basis for later versions

radar: an electronic instrument that uses radio waves to find the distance and location of other objects

radiation: energy given off in the form of waves or very tiny particles

solar cells: a device that converts the energy of sunlight into electric energy

solar system: the Sun together with the eight planets and all other bodies that orbit the Sun

theories: explanations that fit the observed facts

ultraviolet rays: invisible beams of light that are part of the energy that comes from the Sun

Index

airplanes 20

ice 9, 11, 19

Mariner 4 10, 29
Mariner 9 11
Mars Global Surveyor 14
Mars Pathfinder 15, 17, 29, 30
Mars Phoenix 19
Mars Reconnaissance Orbiter 19
Martians 4, 5, 8, 13

NASA 10, 12, 13, 14, 15, 18, 19, 20, 21, 23, 26, 27, 29, 30

Opportunity 18, 19

probe 6, 9, 10, 11, 12, 14, 15, 19, 20, 21, 22, 23, 24, 28, 29

research station 26, 27
robotic moles 21, 29
rover 6, 16, 17, 18, 20, 22, 23, 29

Sojourner 16, 17, 18, 29
Spirit 18, 19

Viking 1 12, 16
Viking 2 12, 16

water 10, 11, 18, 19, 29

ML

12/09